On Tiptoes
In Expectation

On Tiptoes In Expectation

Prayers for Advent,
Christmas,
and Epiphany

Donna Schaper

Abingdon Press
Nashville

ON TIPTOES IN EXPECTATION
PRAYERS FOR ADVENT, CHRISTMAS, AND EPIPHANY

ISBN 0-687-02007-7

03 04 05 06 07 08 09 10 11 12 – 10 9 8 7 6 5 4 3 2 1

MANUFACTURED IN THE UNITED STATES OF AMERICA

To Arnold Kenseth,
a man of fine words

CONTENTS

Advent

ADVENT PRAYERS

In a world where the crack in the sidewalk has become the Grand Canyon, in a world of swirling stocks and sinking bonds, in a world where our very pensions drive globalization and we know we are a part of a new world order not yet yours, not yet holy, come, gentle Jesus, and free us. Come soon, come quiet, come holy. Come small. Come as silently and powerfully as a gene and reshape our destiny, so that the world might be new, might be Holy, might be like you. Amen.

Julia Esquivel, an exiled Guatemalan poet, somewhere today is alive and writing poetry. The Herods are chasing her—and many. O God, keep the hounded safe. Amen.

Born in a manger yet light of the world, born common yet observed by kings, born to center paradox in the deep heart of time and space, come and incarnate in us a troubled spirit, one that looks up, looks around, and sees beyond the surface to the great links between small and large, rich and poor, now and then, time and eternity. Amen.

We spend so much time winging it, blessed Jesus, we forget our focus. We misplace our flight plan. As Advent deepens and your birth comes, reshape us. Renew us. Focus us. Let us not only know you but become like you, now and soon. Amen.

Centers and margins, ins and outs, popular and unpopular, geeks and goons, fat and thin—all of us are yours, O God. Mary and Joseph are as much a part of us as the President and First Lady. This whole ball of wax is one because of you and your entry into history that all may be one. Thanks be to you, O God. Amen.

What love requires of us is to follow your small, marginalized, insignificant way straight to the centers of life and power. Come, Lord Jesus, and show us the way.

Whatever desire possesses us will make us as small as it unless a larger aspiration takes us over. Aspiration can make us as large as desire can make us small. You who messed up the scales: lead us! Cradle by cradle, star by star, step by step—let's go. Amen.

Illuminate our life with a holy star. Light our way. Lighten us. Get us to look up and live, day by day, way by way. Amen.

Spiritual fitness and physical fitness compel us, O God. How did you stay so well, through it all—night journeys and no place to stay. Mix-ups. Missed cues. Angel interruptions. Show us how you have stayed so well. Amen.

❖ ❖ ❖

Horses to automobiles, outdoor to indoor toilets, now spaceships, why is there so much change, so fast? And here it is Advent again. Some of our lights are still up from last year. This year let us really look at those lights. Slow us down. Let us see life as it hums by. Amen.

Mary, were you lonely for a sister or a mother that night? Joseph, were you scared? Jesus, they loved you into life as best they could. You know they did. We love you that way too. Amen.

Confusion and complexity end too many conversations when in fact, like your birth, they might begin them. God become man is confusing; heaven come to earth is as complex a thought as either heaven's cosmos or earth's layers. Let us avoid confusion, embrace complexity, and get on with your loving, simplifying, penetrating to the core. Amen.

Even sneakers aren't easy to wear. But they are comfortable—perhaps too comfortable. Who are you with, O God? The comfortable, or the kids whose feet hurt because they stood all day for thirty cents an hour making the sneakers? Tell us, O God, show us the way to true comfort. Amen.

When next we go to the city to be counted, let us remember that we do count. We do matter. That's why you came to remind us of who counts and what matters. Amen.

So often we can't find the seam. We are less often amazed and more often mazed. Puzzled. A knot is tied and we can't find its clue. Walk with us every day of Advent and out of the maze into the core of your loving life. Seam us to your side, O God. Amen.

Complexity and our complicity in it, chaos and our fuzziness, the upside and downside of globalization—all these matters plague us. Some days we even forget it is Advent. We don't see the candles adding new light each Sunday—but there they are. Love. Faith. Hope. Peace. These certainties assure us now, and in Advent. Amen.

Let us take stock during Advent. Let us become true stakeholders in true value, in the things that grow and the things that matter. And on these things let us earn interest and invest, invest, invest, risk, risk, risk. That's your way. Make it ours. Amen.

When I eat today, let me be grateful. When I sleep today, let me be peaceful. When I walk today, let me be nimble. When I die, take me home with you to Bethlehem and Jerusalem. Amen.

Sustainability is a code word but you lived it. You started small and stayed small, started simple and stayed simple. May we also. Amen.

Bring us to grips with the ground you walked, the long road from Bethlehem to Jerusalem to a Golgotha hill, to an empty tomb. Let us be brave enough to go the whole way with you, from beginning to end. Amen.

Like you, O God, I was a child. Like you, Jesus, I have a mother and father. Like you, I was born with less than I have now. Like you, I have felt very alone. During Advent, let me remember my times and yours. Amen.

We wait for new heavens and a new earth.
—*2 Peter 3:13b NRSV*

Come, thou long-expected Jesus, come as footprints in the snow and show us your way. Thou who brings the scattered home, thou who heals the abandoned senses, thou who brings streams to the desert, come softly to us in this Advent season. Bring us home by your path. Open our eyes and ears. Revive the desert places in us that we may yet blossom. Don't let the world be cold. Don't let the world be dry. But bring your promises close to it.

Freshen it. And let us stand on tiptoes of expectation, daily through Advent, convinced that we will find your footprints on our paths, and that one day soon we will see the new heavens and the new earth as well. With gratitude for your promises, amen.

"For he has regarded the low estate of his handmaiden. . . ."

—*Luke 1:48 RSV*

Holy Spirit, thou who broods over all the space where silence reigns, hear us when we find no words, no justifications, no excuses, only the thud of fact and memory, only the knowledge that too many tables are too thinly laid, that too many fathers drive their children on tires too bald, that even we are poor in ways that frighten us. Come, as you have promised, to the place in us that cannot speak, and stir us up. Stir us up to memory and to hope. Restore our voice to us. Remind us that you have regarded the low estate of many handmaidens. Remind us that you do not put down the poor or the little, but rather exalt us. Break through the drumbeat of violence and poverty and show us ways to raise our small voices to large hopes.

Overcome in us the fear of exposure and let us willingly make the case for the handmaiden, with the handmaiden, that we may in our time know the exaltation of those of low estate, through Jesus Christ our Lord, amen.

And, lo, the angel of the Lord came upon them, and the glory of the Lord shone round about them: and they were sore afraid.

—Luke 2:9 KJV

If we pray for peace, and there is no peace in us, O Lord, still thou wilt hear. If we pray for justice and keep our own fists clenched, O Lord, still thou wilt hear. If we pray for healing, and our bodies turn in toward their own tension, O Lord, still thou wilt heal. And if fear of the unknown gets in the way of our waiting for you, you will send a band of angels. They will watch over us and wait with us until again we are ready to wait for you. Send them now, Lord. Send them now so that fear may turn soon to rejoicing. In the name of the Babe, amen.

. . . and heaven and nature sing.

—UMH 246

Sometimes we scurry so for joy that we forget what it feels like. Sometimes we work so hard for peace that we neglect the peace that is sitting with us in our chair. Sometimes we hope so much for hope that we miss the hopeful signs that are right underfoot. Give us this day, a song, one we sing in harmony with heaven and nature. Let the song recollect joy, be peace itself, let the song hope a little ahead of our own hope. You grant us joy and peace and hope: these are not our own accomplishments. Let this day find us, with heaven and with nature, singing about you. Through Jesus Christ, our Lord. Amen.

For lo! the days are hastening on. . . .

—UMH 218

We come as a people nearly weary with hope, having waited too long, and ashamed of our weariness. We know how long you have waited: waited for us to come to our senses; waited for us to acknowledge rainbows, tablets, red seas parted—one sign after another. Now instead of being weary you send one more Sign. This time a baby, one who sneaks into our world almost silently. Remind us this day that the days are hastening on. That what the prophets foretold is soon to be true. And gather and focus our attention on the manger. This time, let your people see your sign. Amen.

O little town of Bethlehem . . .

We are amazed at Bethlehem. It is so small and so insignificant, so much like the places we live in or where we were born. It seems nearly impossible that you could use it for your grand historical purposes. But if you can, that means you can use us too. If Bethlehem is worthy, then so perhaps are we. Come now, into our quiet space and into our little town, and point us to your purpose. Thanks be to you, O God. Amen.

Ancient of Days, whose glory the cradle tells, whose hope the star displays, whose love the birth confirms, guide us now by the light of the star. Let us forsake the romance of moonlight, the plans we had to be our own selves, all that we would ever need. Let us regard less the pragmatism of sunlight, that the ways of this world would be adequate to the ways you had in mind originally. Let us be wild in our hopes by starlight, that AIDS will be cured, that peace will splatter all the earth, that we ourselves will calm down in midnights clear, that our children will pick up their toys. Let the star show us how mountains will be brought low and valleys raised up, how in the small we will find the large. Take the mountain part of us and bring it low, take the valley part and lift it up. Let us follow your star. Amen.

On this day, earth shall ring.

—UMH 248

Holy Spirit, living God, if we listen with you today we can almost hear the packages rustling, the ribbons blowing, the children squealing. If we listen with you, we hear the church bells ringing, the choirs singing, the whole bright world less heavy, just by virtue of this day. Many of us don't even know why. We just know that the day is meant for lightness, meant to mention Christ, made to help us remember that we were not put on this great big planet alone, or without comfort. On this day our warfare has ended. God is with us. We are not alone. A Child is born. Thanks and praises. Amen.

Ancient of Days, who comes to us fresh as tomorrow and sure as dawn's bump of the horizon in early light, draw near now and wait with us. Wait for the return of glory, the advent of holy time, the birth of a child. Wait with us for the end of our regret, the rebirth of our joy, the time when old becomes new before our very eyes.

Renew us. Give us patience. Let us remember how sure it is that weeping only endures for the night and joy returns in the morning. Let us remember the depth of our sadness on other occasions, and how surely you bring us back to gladness.

Give this congregation the patience of Advent, that we may be confident of Christmas but not rush it. Let time slow down now, and, in holy patience, let us await you and your entrance into history, even our own. Amen.

There is a little bit of saint in each of us, O God, and a little bit of sinner. You know this already.

You know our comings out and our goings in. You know because it is in you that we live and move and have our very being.

This day, we pray that saint may edge out sinner, that we may find ourselves stretched toward you and not pushed away. We pray that we may become all that you made us and that we may give honor to our creation. We pray that we not become "holier than thou" so much as holy. That we become not perfect, but instead the best that we can be.

Stay with us, O God. Don't go far away. Keep your Holy Spirit nearby, as near as it was to the cradle of your Son, as close to our bed as breath. Amen.

Luminescence and Joy, Holy God, Light of Lights and Very God of Very God, draw near and light our path. Remind us that we can't really see beyond our own headlights and that we don't need to see any further. Let us be glad to see what we can see, and let us know that it is your light that gives us sight. Take away the worry that we can't plan everything or know everything. Let what comes, come. In the name of your coming, amen.

(The following is a five-part prayer for the lighting of the Advent candles. Each Sunday features a reading by a leader and a family or individual. Following the readings for Sunday Five is a congregational litany that can be used each Sunday. Each meditation includes a time of silence for a guided meditation, a time when the pastor simply opens the door on a subject and gives the congregation permission to meditate.)

Sunday One

Leader: So little is clear. So much is fuzzy. Bring us to clarity, God. Lift one layer of confusion and clutter so that we may see. Show us how we use confusion to keep from moving. Give us a deeper appreciation of complexity—and from there let us see all the lights that you have placed at the end of our tunnel.

Family or Individual One: I light this first Advent candle in honor of simplicity and its partner, complexity. I pray for clarity.

Pastor: Meditate on the hard and confusing parts of your life in the silence that comes—and then imagine a clearing in a forest. After two minutes, I will say "Amen."

Sunday Two

Leader: Many people are lost. Many are in exile. Many are far from home. Remind us of all the times we have been lost before—and of all the times you have already found us. Through Jesus Christ our Path and Core, amen.

Family or Individual Two: I light this second Advent candle in honor of our homes. I pray for a home for everyone in the world.

Pastor: Meditate on the front door to your home. After two minutes, I will say "Amen."

Sunday Three

Leader: Even though it is Advent, and the candlelight is gathering around, heading toward its Christmas fullness, still many of us are rushing around, fearing that we aren't doing all we should. Remind us of the pressures we have already faced in our lives, remind us of last Christmas and how everything does come out fine in the end. In the name of the Center and Source of this holy season, Jesus Christ, amen.

Family or Individual Three: I light this third Advent candle in honor of quietness. I pray for quietness for every person in the world, especially for those who are especially harried.

Pastor: Meditate on the last Christmas tree you had in your home or saw and liked. Appreciate it. After two minutes, I will say "Amen."

Sunday Four

Leader: The fullness of time now comes. We move to the center of history and the center of life in the birth of Jesus Christ. We are no longer outsiders but insiders to the mystery of the world. Come, Holy Spirit, and in the long pause before the fourth candle is lit, awaken in us a real hunger for peace, our peace and the peace of your whole world.

Family or Individual Four: I light this fourth candle to honor the center of our lives and our history, Jesus Christ. I light slowly, taking all the time in the world, because that is what we have, here and now.

Sunday Five

Leader: Joy has come to the world in the baby Jesus. Joy came through Bethlehem, a little place, an ordinary place, to ordinary people who didn't think that much of themselves. That means joy can come also to us. Come, Lord Jesus, be our guest. Let thy gift to us be blessed.

Family or Individual Five: I light these five candles because of joy—joy in clarity, joy in homes, joy in quietness, joy in the center of time and space, which is Jesus Christ, our Lord.

Congregational Litany

For the light of personal clarity,
   we give you thanks, O God.
For the light of our homes,
   we give you thanks, O God.
For the light of quiet times,
   we give you thanks, O God.
For the light of inner peace,
   we give you thanks, O God.
For the light of joy,
   we give you thanks, O God.

(The following are guided meditations for the congregation for the lighting of the Advent candles. These may be combined with the previous lightings or kept separate as a second alternative.)

Candle One

Leader: In Advent, we come to a clearing in the great forest of our days. There is a glow. It is from God. Let us find our way to the clearing today. Let us see the rest of our day from its perspective. In the name of your creation and the purpose for which you made us, amen.

> *(Meditation One: As one candle is lit, people are encouraged to guide their meditation toward a picture of a clearing in the forest. If audiovisuals are available, a clearing would be a good picture to show.) (Each member of the congregation who wants to come forward during the quiet meditation and extinguish and relight the candle should be free to do so. Quiet music should be played. The meditation should go on for two minutes or so, focusing on its own silence and the "great clearing in the forest of our days.")*

Closing prayer: We stand in the great clearing, O God, the one you make every week in worship for us. Send us back to our forests, invigorated, lightened, and ready for all that comes our way.

Candle Two

Leader: Gracious God, my life forms a circle whose center is Spirit. Flood it with light. Fill it with grace. Make it a beautiful shape, the kind people will see and remember and want to be like themselves. Let it be the right size, not too big and not too small. Let its light shine on others' paths—without diminishing its own. Let it be one of those lamps whose oil never empties, and let those who dwell within its circle be safe and secure from all harm. Let it be one of those circles that can't be broken. Let everything you put together not be torn asunder. In the name of the safety known as salvation, the safety known as security, the certainty of light, amen.

(As candle two is lit, the members of the congregation are encouraged to think about their own lives and their circles and to give thanks for the relationships they have, both those that are whole and those that are broken.)
(Congregants may be free to come forward to light a candle on a table. Candles should be provided. If dozens are lit, great; if not, that is also fine. Think of a European cathedral where many candles are available.)

Closing Prayer to the Meditation: Remind us that the days are hastening on, that what the prophets foretold is soon to be true. And gather and focus our attention on the manger. This time, let your people see your sign. And let the sign of your manger also be the sign of our life. Amen.

Candle Three

Litany

Reader 1: I will light a light in the name of God, who lit the world and breathed the breath of life into it.

Reader 2: I will light a light in the name of the Spirit, whose fire burns bright and blesses my soul with yearning.

Reader 3: I will light a light in the name of the Christ, whose fire burns clear and blesses my soul with focus.

ALL: We will light three lights for the Trinity of love: God above us, God beside us, God beneath us—the beginning, the end, the everlasting one.

Congregation sings:

This little light of mine, I'm goin' to let it shine, let it shine, let it shine.

Don't let Satan blow it out, I'm goin' to let it shine.

Hide it under a bushel? No, I'm goin' to let it shine.

Let it shine till justice comes; I'm goin' to let it shine.

(This above lighting is adapted from Iona Community Peace Institute, Glasgow, Scotland.)

Candle Four

Four people light four candles with these words:

I light this candle in honor of the small.

I light this candle in honor of children.

I light this candle in honor of those who are poor.

I light this candle in the name of those who think they are small.

Meditation: Please think about something small; love it and honor it. After two minutes, the pastor will say "Amen."

Closing prayer together: We are amazed at Bethlehem sometimes, O God. It is so small and so insignificant, so much like the places where we live or were born. It seems nearly impossible that you could use it for your grand historical purposes. But if you can, that means you can use us. If Bethlehem is worthy, then so perhaps are we. Come now into our quiet space and into our little town, and point us to the purposes you have. Why are we here? To what end have you dedicated us? On this day make a little sense of our lives. Thanks be to you, O God. Amen.

Candle Five

As five youth light the candles on the wreath, each says one of the following lines:

I light this candle in honor of stars.
I light this candle in honor of galaxies.
I light this candle in honor of telescopes.
I light this candle in honor of meteors.
I light this candle in honor of the light that comes in the night.

> *(The meditation is on the subject of stars. Graphics or visuals of stars could be used, if available. After two minutes of meditation, the pastor will say "Amen.")*

Family or Individual: Ancient of Days, whose glory the cradle tells, whose hope the star displays, whose love the birth confirms, guide us now by the light of the Star. Let us forsake the romance of moonlight, the plans we had to be our own selves all that we would ever need. Let us regard less the pragmatism of sunlight, that the ways of this world would be adequate to the Ways you had in mind originally. Let us be wild in our hopes by Starlight, that peace will splatter all the earth. Let the Star show us how mountains will be brought low and valleys will be raised up, how in the small we will find the large.

An Advent Blessing

O Great One,
Spirit of the living God,
Fiery, sweeping power of love,
Rest your love upon each one now.
Rest your love upon each woman,
Upon each man,
Upon your sons and daughters of this passage.

Move with them,
Move with them in their journey from here

To where your call leads them,
Move with them to some yet unlived life, wrapped
  in mystery.
Give them something for their journey.
Give them language
To speak love in a thousand ways,
A liberating love
Far wider than we imagined.

Speak your Word, O great One,
A Word-made-Flesh.
Speak your Word through them
Body and soul,
In touch
With the ordinary,
With the broken,
With the lost.

Speak your liberating Word-made-Flesh in them,
Like Jesus,
Loving the ordinary,
Healing the broken,
Finding the lost.

Rest meaning upon each one, O great One,
Spirit of the living God,
Fiery, sweeping power of love.

Prayers for the Ordinary Days of Advent

Beat in our hearts and souls and wombs, O God. Beat out the rhythm of calm and safety and salvation. Let us all hear the beat together. Amen.

Let gladness break with morning today, O God. Wait with me for the right moment to do the hard thing I must do today. Remove the grudge I have against it and allow me to learn from it. Let me have done with lesser things. Take me off schedule in some good way and surprise me with the partnership that allows difficulty to be entered with hope. In Jesus' name, amen.

O Flower of Jesse's stem, you whom we confuse with Christmas bonuses and bright shiny boxes, you who are as present in June as in January, on paycheck days as on Christmas, you who came to incarnate the right kind of appreciation of the material, let this day be good because of the money we earn. And let it be also more than the money we earn. Teach us this truth: nothing here below is profane for those who know how to see. Through the Incarnate Christ, amen.

You are the wall-stone, O God, and I the builder. As beautiful as the walls lay on the barren fields in winter, so was our work together today. Stone by stone, connection by connection, arrangement by arrangement, lift by lift, each move had beauty. I give thanks that I was able to make moves. To haul. To connect. To arrange. Let what we did today endure. Let it make many generations glad. Let it be beautiful. In the name of those who build houses and all who build churches and all who build circuits, and all who make connections. In the name of your Son, who is the very foundation and cornerstone, amen.

Rebuild what is broken, O God, and use me to repair it. Restore streets to dwell in. Let the ancient city return to us in all its glory. And receive the offering of what I did today, as part of your grand project. A small part. But a part nonetheless. Through Jesus Christ, amen.

For the unemployed, I pray: that they find jobs, that they find hope to find jobs, that they find good jobs, that they not be afraid. And that I do to them what I would have them do to me were our situations reversed. In the name of Jesus and the golden rule, amen.

Christmas

CHRISTMAS PRAYERS

Christmas Eve

Midnight has cleared before our very eyes, and your holy child is bringing an uncommon light into the world. Thanks be to you, O God, who knows so well the way of light and darkness and assures us of the light. Thanks be to you, O God, who knows the power of the small, the bliss of Bethlehem, the extraordinary of the ordinary. Here you come, in normal time, to do a marvelous thing. For the choice of a child to save us, we praise your holy Name.

Let this night contain the kind of memory that lasts. Candlelight, greens, mangers far away—let each remind us of you as the year progresses. Let each straw in the manger represent a holy respect for you that is borne by millions around the world this sacred night. Blend our hearts with hearts of those everywhere who rejoice in your time and your coming into our time.

Let the people join together in glad *Amen.*

Holy Breath, holy Spirit, you who move so lightly on wave and wind, you who can be as mighty as a hurricane, as strong as a tornado, draw near. Give us light. Give us hope. Give us spirit. Let us be strong and tender simultaneously, even as you are. Let us be fierce in defending the gospel and humble in our understandings of its completeness.

Let us join people of all time in awe and wonder and let us become the kind of people they were—real, awed, full, capable, despite weakness, of great witness. When we lose our way, guide us. When we are winded, invigorate us. When we go too far on too little, companion us. Never let us be far from our source in you. And astound us with the mighty Trinity this Christmas Eve, the one whose word became flesh and now dwells among us, by the mighty power of the Spirit of God, the One whose and whom you are. Amen.

Like the Gambian who thought his car had been painted white when it snowed, we stand in awe at what your birth means, holy Jesus. Like the African who had never seen snow before, we run out of our classroom and roll in the news of something pure and holy and good come to us. Like the young girl from Miami who goes to school in the North, we delight in the crystalline beauty of your coming to us. Snowy emmanuel, bless us as we rejoice in your blessing. Amen.

(The following prayer is suitable for a communion service on Christmas Eve.)

A bit of bread and a bit of wine, a small blessing and the invocation of the Holy Spirit and next thing we know we are standing on holy ground, eating at a holy table, communing with our Christ. This is not magic so much as depth, not mysterious so much as normal. Life is food at the table with our Lord. A simple meal is also a holy meal; a holy meal is also a simple meal. We are one with each other at this table and one with our God.

Let your Holy Spirit come. Let us give thanks. The feast is ready. What began with a small child is the fullest of divine incarnations. Feed us, O God, and here set us free to understand your world and your word as incarnate. Amen.

Bless by the power of your Holy Spirit, gracious God, the children, family, and individuals gathered here tonight. Let them know the paradoxical meaning of innocence, that we are both wise as serpents and innocent as doves. Let each of them be assured of your intention for our maturation. We are not to be children forever. But sometimes being an adult is so hard. Stay with us, O God. Don't go far. This baby needs help. And you give us all the help we need. Let us mature. Let us become adults as the Christ Child did—without losing the joy of being your children. Thanks be to you, O God. Amen.

On this holy night we remember all people who have died in this year. We remember those who have lost a loved one and who know an acute loneliness this night. And we remember all who have given birth this year. We remember all who have wandered to a far country and there stood up and were counted.

We give you thanks, O God, for this great country,

for its North and South, East and West, for its mountains and rivers, trees and forests. We give you thanks for the hopes it has, of liberty and justice for all. We give you thanks for all that it is not yet and pray for the day when the country realizes its fondest dreams of democracy and liberty and justice.

In the Christmas story we find our story, both its nature and its grace. Let us see tonight. Let us see all the way to the end of the story, the end of time, the connections between life and death. Guide us to true wisdom, the wisdom of a baby in a manger. Amen.

On a night of such abundance, it is very difficult to remember those who are homeless, those who are alone, those who don't care anymore. And yet, you would remember them, O God. In fact, you sent your son so that those who mourn would never be without a friend. For that act, we praise you and pray for the day when our memories can be as good as yours. Send us out with some kindness tonight. Send us out with enough freedom from our own wealth, whatever it is, that we can give it away. And bless our journey, that it takes us to those you especially love. Amen.

Some of us have too much. And others have too little. And your sure intention is that we each have all that we need. That we learn not to want what others have. That instead we learn to want what we do have.

Deepen the everyday grace at our table this holiday and holy day. Let us know our daily food as manna, as miracle, as abundance. Let us know our daily rest as life-giving. Let us remember each member of our family as a beautiful facet of your creation, even those from whom we are estranged.

Hear our thanks for our church, our pastors, our musicians, our custodians—all who help us worship together and who keep things working here.

And, finally, O God, hear our prayer for those who don't have enough. Let us play our part in the return of their abundance. Amen.

In this great silent night, we dig deep into our pockets for a gift that will be the size of you. If we are not ready now, let us be ready soon to mark your incarnation in our world with a gift that is the size of our gratitude to you. Amen.

Christmas Day

J oy has come to the world, peace has come on earth, we need worry no more. Immanuel, God be with us, we have prayed for so long, and now God is here. In the serendipity and surprise of a child, in the wonder of two young parents, in the wisdom of sages and the humility of shepherds, in innkeepers who make room when there is no room, in all these narratives and more, we know your presence among us.

Let us not forget, as gorgeous papers and ribbons clutter our living rooms, what we know here and now. The ultimate gift is your child: Christ is born in Bethlehem, wrapped in the normal blankets of a normal child, yet containing deep within the genetics of joy, the seeds of peace, the DNA of salvation.

Bless our own gift giving that it too be marked with joy and filled with peace. Let our gratitude to others show, and let it come straight from our gratitude for you. In the name of the child, amen.

S how forth, O God, in power and peace what you have done and are doing in our world. Before some of us can sing a song of gladness again, O God, we have to get over something. We have a fear of your story, an estrangement from it. Some of us are angry. Some of us are hurt. And no one seems to notice. They keep telling us everything is going to be all right, but still we're hurt. Help us tell the truth without making people even more afraid of us. And on this Christmas Day let the joy that comes be real. Let it ping like fine crystal. May the phony be banned on behalf of the real, in and through us, and show us the way. In the name of your authentic Son and his very real birth, amen.

Reveal yourself, O God, to each one of us here. Bring us to your glory and on to new days. In the name of Jesus, who never goes far. Let us marvel like shepherds and rejoice like angels. Let us rest with Mary and Joseph, who still have a long way to go on their journey home. As we open our gifts, may we remember your gift, its holiness and its abundance. And may we fall asleep tonight in deep thanksgiving that a star has come our way. Amen.

Hibernating animals join people who need to slow down now, O God. The short days remind us of the need to sleep. They also beckon us to warm fires and rocking chairs and places of comfort. Let what we do in this season be a sign of warmth to the cold world.

Let us love our sweaters and our boots and our jackets. Let us love the way you made the world, as a place that changes and is almost never repetitive, one day after the other. Let us love the big storms and the little storms, those in life and those in weather.

And keep the words of complaint far from our lips. In the name of Jesus, amen.

Today, O God, open our eyes and ears. Revive the desert places in us that we may yet blossom. Don't let the world be cold. Don't let the world be dry. But bring your promises close to it. Freshen it. And let us stand on tiptoes of expectation, daily through Advent, convinced that we will find your footprints on our paths, and that one day soon we will see these gifts blossom as flowers in the desert.

Rumors of angels abound. These rumors are magnificent. They make us feel like Mary, so full and round with joy, so fully glad to be herself even if she couldn't understand what all was happening. Still she knew the glow of your spirit, your angels, your promise coming true. Make us likewise pregnant with joy as the light comes to us, as slow as a birth and just as sure. Amen.

N ow let thy servants depart in peace, according to your holy word. Now also let this blessed year depart in its own peace. Let it become a part of the centuries, and let us give thanks that we were privileged to live in it, through it, and by it. As we turn the page on your calendar, and remember to add a new date to our checks and letters, move with us, O God. Stay close by. Let us not get confused about whose is whose and what is what. Let us remember you as the source of our years and our days. And let this last week of the year be special to us in memory and as hope, even as you chose to begin time with one child and one birth. Let this time be holy to us, filled with the power of your presence, amen.

O n this day of many packages and much jubilation, we pray today for a great cleaning out of the closet. We need to let go of the hurt we sometimes enjoy carrying around. Someday order will return to this chaos, and we will be proud of the stuff that has started to chase us. Between now and then, when we see our lives, let us love them like the day we opened our first Christmas package, the day we first knew that Jesus Christ is Lord, the day we first met the babe and knew that divinity lurked there.

Let what we give and receive be a holy reminder of all you are to us, both now and for all the days to come. In your chaos, may we see heaven. In your clarity, may we be relieved of confusion enough to know our life's center is in you and your holy story. Amen.

Epiphany

EPIPHANY PRAYERS

You whose power is love and whose love is power. You who know the strength in weakness, the face in vulnerability, you have come to us as a child. May we be wise enough to understand what this means.

Without darkness, the poet tells us, we wouldn't be able to see the stars. We need our trouble to see the light. Let us appreciate the way you used the star to show us Jesus—and let us come to pay more attention to stars. Amen.

The earth moves under our feet, the sky comes falling down—shift is everywhere—but your son remains the same, today, tomorrow, and yesterday, a fixed point in a changing world. He is a child, a word become flesh, a mysterious center to all of time. We love him and pray to understand him soon.

When our days try to turn into fragments of meaningless pieces and our nights are long and restless, gather us, O God, back at the manger. These remind us of what it's all about—you and your love for the world. Don't let us forget the way the faithful gathered on Christmas Eve—and lit candles that centered us and the world. Amen.

We wake, we sleep, we wander through our days. You, O God, perhaps do the same— you rest, you work, you enter our history, our time and space. We learn to love you the way you first loved us. Thanks be to you, O God. Amen.

Time is your habitation, O God. You are eternity come into calendar at Christmas. Now it is Epiphany, and your spirit grows slowly within us. Amen.

We come to the end of the birth and the beginning of all time, the end of the beginning of time—and we wait with joy for an epiphany. We wait to know what the birth of this baby means for us and for history. Bring us to slow awakening and to true meaning—but let us not be greedy. Let us learn slowly and carefully so that we do not miss anything. Let our knowledge of you grow embryo-like, childlike, just as you so gently have come among us. Amen.

*E*piphanos, the making manifest, the showing forth, the coming together of end and beginning—thanks be to you, O God, for all that you do for us and to us, for all the beauty you place before our eyes and for all you intend for us. Be with us in this season and let us comprehend the birth of your Son. Let us change our lives because of it—and grow in us now. Amen.

A great awakening is before us. We may now truly live, truly grow up, truly be free. The reason is your love for us, O God. Hear our amazement and our joy—and also bring us childlike to a state of alert attention, one that salutes you and our salvation and your Son. Amen.

Wise men stand on tiptoes; those of us not so learned join them—and we let amazement cover us head to toe. How can God come as a child and how can a child be God? We stand amazed and wear awe as our garment. Be with us and let calm return to our homes after the magnificence of the Christmas eruption. Let the calm marry the amazement and make us new. Amen.

When terror strikes and fear overtakes, when life makes no sense, when even Christmas gifts lose their shine, and we fight extra pounds along with deep fear, draw us back to the manger, that place where we fear not and simply behold. There let us rest, there let us know peace—there let us know you. Amen.

Angels and shepherds are less in the news these days; we have moved to the let-down stage. The pack-up-the-decorations stage. The buy-cheap-paper-for-next-year stage. No more feast, we're back to food. But inside us burns a flame, small as a remembered candle, strong as a forest fire. We know what you have done and we will not forget. The child is born within us. Amen.